The Clouds Float North

MW00452888

This book was supported by a grant from the
Eric Mathieu King Fund of The Academy of American Poets.

The Clouds Float North

The Complete Poems of Yu Xuanji

BILINGUAL EDITION

Translated by David Young and Jiann I. Lin

Wesleyan University Press

Middletown, Connecticut

Wesleyan University Press

Middletown, CT 06459

www.wesleyan.edu/wespress

Collection and translations © 1998 by David Young and Jiann I. Lin

All rights reserved

Printed in the United States of America

CIP data appear at the end of the book

ISBN-13: 978-0-8195-6344-6

Acknowledgment

Some of these poems appeared first in *FIELD*, and we are grateful for permission to reprint them.

Frontispiece

Yun Bing, Chinese, active 1670–1710, *Peonies and Garden Rock*. Allen Memorial Art Museum, Oberlin College, Ohio. Mary McClure Bequest, 1945. © Allen Memorial Art Museum.

CONTENTS

Yu Xuanji: An Introduction • ix

•

Poem for the Willows by the River • 1

Sent to a Neighbor Woman Friend • 2

The Fragrance of Orchids • 3

Tribute to a Master Alchemist • 4

Sent to Secretary Liu • 5

Washing Yarn Temple • 7

Selling the Last Peonies • 8

To Thank the Scholar Li for the Gift of a Bamboo Mat • 9

Love Letter to Li Zian • 10

Boudoir Bitterness • 11

Spring Thoughts Sent Affectionately to Zian • 13

Watching Them Play Polo • 15

Sent to a Friend in a Late Spring Mood • 16

Sent to Wen Feiqing on a Winter Night • 17

A Poem Sent to Li Ying to Match His "Fishing in Summer" • 18

Matching Poem for My New Neighbor to the West,
Inviting Him over for Wine • 19

A Matching Poem, Reply to a Friend • 20

Two Poems • 21

Visiting the South Pavilion at Chongzhen Temple Where
the Civil Service Exam Results Are Posted • 23

Melancholy Thoughts • 24

Autumn Lament • 25

River Journey • 26

Hearing Squire Li Had Gone Fishing, I Sent Him This Poem • 27

The Zifu Temple, Founded by the Hermit Ren • 28

The Yinwu Pavilion • 29

The Double Ninth Festival Delayed by Rain • 30

Early Autumn • 31

Remembering Strong Emotions • 32

For a Friend Who Didn't Arrive Because of Heavy Rain • 34

Visiting Master Zhao and Not Finding Him • 35

Curing Yourself When Lovesick • 36

Sent to Feiqing • 38

Visiting Ezhou • 39

Living in the Mountains in Summer • 40

Late Spring Improvisation • 41

Joining Somebody's Mourning • 42

Letter to a Friend • 43

Sent to Zian, Long Distance, from the Hanjiang River • 44

An Allegory • 45

Letter to Zian, Sad from Gazing into the Distance, from Jiangling • 46

Sent to Zian • 47

Saying Goodbye • 48

A Warm Note to Squire Li Jinren • 49

Saying Goodbye, II • 50

Letter to an Exam Candidate, from Shanxi to the Capital • 51

Reply to a Poem, Matching the Form • 53

Three Beautiful Sisters, Orphaned Young • 54

Snapping Willows • 57

Fragments • 58

•

Notes • 61

YU XUANJI

An Introduction

Outside her remarkable poems, we know very little about Yu Xuanji. Her surname, Yu, which means "fish," is unusual. Her given name, Xuanji (Hsüanchi in Wade–Giles romanization), means something like "dark secret" or "mysterious luck." She was born around 844 and died around 871, at the age of twenty-eight. One source describes her life and work this way:

> A woman of the Tang Dynasty (618–907), from Chang'an; byname 'Youwei;' second byname 'Huilan.' She was fond of study and had some talent. She became a lesser wife of the official Li Yi [Li Zian]. The love between them decayed, and Xuanji became a Daoist [Taoist] nun in the Xian Yi Temple. Because a novice died from a beating administered by Xuanji for disciplinary reasons, Xuanji herself was condemned and executed. She left one book of poems. (Gwoyeu Tsyrdean [*A Dictionary of the National Language*])

Her bynames, or "courtesy names" (which are like nicknames, but more formal), mean, in the first case, "young and tiny" or "young and profound," and, in the second case, "orchid." The name of the temple she went to suggests something like "All Suitable" or "Just As It Should Be."

Western role names like "nun" and "concubine" (lesser wife) and "courtesan" (since a number of the poems suggest that she led this life as well) are clumsy ways at best of denoting social roles and relationships that were very different from the ones we know. They fail to characterize a life that we are more likely to glimpse, if we manage it at all, by turning to the remarkable poems she left, forty-nine in number. These poems reflect her relations with men—relations that are certainly more complex and interesting than any reduction of them to sex and commercial transaction would suggest—and they also show her exploring the Daoist ideals of meditation, solitude, and contemplation of nature. Behind them stands a person who escapes stereotypes, a gifted writer who explores the limited options available to her, material and spiritual, with vigor and imagination.

We owe the survival of these poems to the ancient Chinese anthologists' urge to be complete. To their comprehensive period anthologies of what they thought counted most—the poems of men who were also government officials of varying degrees of importance—they couldn't resist adding curiosities: poems by ghosts, poems by monks, priests, and foreigners, even poems by women "and others whose efforts," as *The Indiana Companion to Traditional Chinese Literature* notes, "might provide amusement."

So it was that Yu Xuanji's forty-nine poems survived. The story of her "murder" and "execution" was recounted some twelve years after her death, and it is told, the same source notes, "in such dramatic detail that its historical accuracy becomes suspect." *The Little Tablet from Three Rivers,* source of the tale, sounds a little like the contemporary equivalent of a tabloid. What the truth of this story is, we can never know. Anyone who has seen the recent Chinese film *Raise the Red Lantern* will have some idea of how the intrigues, betrayals, oppressions, and frustrations to which women were subjected in that culture could lead quite plausibly either to a false accusation or to an act of revenge. It is very difficult to reconcile the person behind these poems with a beating that resulted in a death, but it is not impossible, given human nature. What seems equally likely is that the story is apocryphal, or that Yu Xuanji was falsely accused.

We think of women as having been consistently oppressed in ancient China, subjected to rules of modesty and behavior that kept them uneducated, restricted to the household, and unable to think of themselves as gifted individuals—artists, philosophers, composers, or the like. That is far too monolithic a conception of the social and psychological reality. Rhythms of conservatism and liberality have characterized Chinese life as much as they have any other culture. The notorious practice of foot binding, for example, did not become widespread until considerably later, in the Song Dynasty (960–1279). In that same era, however, there were many regions in which it was common for daughters to inherit property, making generalizations about the restrictions and freedoms women suffered and enjoyed quite difficult.

Whether women were educated depended partly on their family and class. In a family of means, all it took was a tolerant and encouraging male or two for this to happen. Whether women were sequestered at home was mostly a class issue, too. Peasant women, for example, were not subject to the same rules and restraints, and women who lived in marginal communities—which would define both the Daoist "nuns" among whom Yu Xuanji lived and the courtesans, who usually had their own districts and domiciles, along with a degree of social freedom that came at the cost of respectability—could take more initiative concerning their own lives and behavior.

In fact, the Tang Dynasty happens to have been a time when women had greater freedom of choice and social mobility than was the case both earlier and later. This had partly to do with the character and lineage of the ruling Li family, and partly to do with the widespread interest in Daoism, which had become the official state religion. Daoist philosophy has always emphasized equality of being—that is why it merged well with Buddhism—and thus acted as a counterweight to Confucianism, whose rules of behavior and decorum were used to keep women tightly restricted to their households, minimally educated, and in contact mostly with just their own immediate families.

What is striking about Yu Xuanji, then, is that in her short and sad life she tried at least three of the available roles by which women could hope to experiment with accomplishments normally associated with male pursuits. She was a concubine in a family where her literary talents were admired and encouraged; she was a Daoist "nun" in a community where concentration on spiritual and intellectual issues was part of the way of life; and she was, apparently, a courtesan, which meant she could associate with well-to-do men, many of them highly educated and powerful, who might well appreciate her spirit and literary accomplishments as much as her personal attractiveness. We are not sure of the order and duration of these roles, but we can see from her poems that each role gave her a valuable perspective on life, and that no one of them could suffice by itself to make her the poet she became. If the sequence was from a wife to a nun/courtesan, as seems likely, even that was fortuitous: first grounding her in the literary tradition she would practice, and then freeing her to move around in her world, meeting male writers and cultivating her mind and her social talents.

To these changes of fortune and situation, then, we owe our sense of the range of her poetry, emotionally and experientially. Missing her husband, flirting with other writers and with lovers, and pondering spiritual truths and accomplishments—these are her poetic stock-in-trade, and their variety gives her poetry a scope and interest it might have lacked had her social options been more limited by a life lived on the terms of a single role.

The variety did not lead, however, to literary fame or full entry to the select circle of top literary talents, even though she knew and corresponded with some of them. Subsequent readers and commentators have not quite known what to make of a writer who had such a short life, such diverse social roles, and whose "career" was crowned with the accusation of blood guilt. The best-known anthology of Tang Dynasty poems, the one that has become a standard "Golden Treasury" of that period, includes work by women poets—more orthodox figures, it should be noted—but not by Yu Xuanji. To the drawback of her gender and her truncated career, we can add the problem of her shifting identity.

All this would seem to suggest that a dominant melancholy surrounds her person and her poems. Yet poets, as cases as diverse as those of Emily Dickinson and Dante Alighieri demonstrate, often thrive on disadvantages and setbacks. The odd thing is that reading Yu Xuanji's poems does not tend to underline the pathos and poignancy of her life; on the contrary, it tends to contradict such responses. What surfaces again and again is a vivid sensibility, expressing itself by full and playful participation in a rich poetic tradition. The complexity and concentration of these poems remind us that Yu Xuanji benefited enormously from coming of age in one of the richest literary periods any culture has ever known. The bonds of convention and artificial diction that had characterized earlier poetry had been thoroughly broken by her seventh-century predecessors, and the directness, realism, and complex tonality that characterize the great achievement of Tang Dynasty poetry were hers for the taking. No one could refuse her this inspiring heritage on the basis of gender or social position. It belonged to any talented writer who cared to take it up.

Many of the poems, to be sure, dwell on absence, longing, and loss, as do lyric poems in any culture and period. But their original handling of theme, their inspired sense of detail, their exuberant rightness of tone and form, all counterbalance the painful subject matter with exquisite formal and aesthetic pleasure. Whether this sleight-of-hand fully compensates the poet is not the question: the reader's gift is the distillation of experience, still potent after eleven centuries. In that distillation, the resilience and dignity of the human spirit are held in a kind of suspension. The pain and pleasure mingle, not canceling each other out but simply coexisting. Two truths are told at once—that life is streaked with sorrow and loss, and that existence is a miraculous gift to the responsive spirit.

Chinese poetry, despite the comparative liberations of the Tang era, is nothing if not conventional. It is far less anxious than the poetry of our own time about achieving originality, and vast tracts of it, virtually indistinguishable, now lie unconsulted in those huge anthologies. Where it survives and our interest is piqued, its special pleasures are those of seeing what can be done with yet another variation on some very familiar theme: the letter of apology or invitation, the reconciliation of turbulent feelings within a tranquil or majestic landscape, the visit to a special place or person, the commemoration of a season's passing, the standard complaints about bad weather, solitude, and separation. It may well be that Yu Xuanji, from her marginal situations and her more oblique relation to what was mainly a pastime of highly educated males, was able to work her variations on these familiar themes with greater flexibility and originality. This would give her something in common with unorthodox careers like those of Li Bai (Li Po) and Li He (Li Ho), poets whose existence outside the government bureaucracy marked them as nonconformists and enhanced their ability to vary norms and depart from conventions.

Indeed, while there are times when she naturally complains about the hardship of combining poetic talent and womanhood, there are also times when Yu Xuanji seems to sense what we might call the advantage of her disadvantages. She is able to adopt a more teasing and playful stance toward other poets, her male friends, and lovers, because of her odd relation to them as both a fellow writer and an object of desire. Her womanhood disables her from certain kinds of fame, position, and company, but it also affords her the opportunity for the lyric transformation of pain into pleasure, loss into consolation.

A closer consideration of her choices of subject is informative because she often writes in response to a specific incident or situation, an occasion. We can think of classical Chinese poetry as *occasional*—written for and in response to a specific occasion—in at least four typical ways: (1) the address to a specific person, usually in the form of a letter; (2) the commemoration of a visit to a special place; (3) the marking of a particular event, such as a death, a victory, or an anniversary; and (4) the portrait of a specific (and also often typical) individual. Yu Xuanji's ease with each of these categories is clear in, respectively, "Love Letter to Li Zian" (p. 10), "The Zifu Temple" (p. 28), "Joining Somebody's Mourning" (p. 42), and "Tribute to a Master Alchemist" (p. 4). These categories of occasional poem are by no means mutually exclusive—a letter may commemorate a visit or a death, for example—but they help to show us the patterns of composition that Yu Xuanji practiced.

The largest number of her "occasional" poems constitute addresses to individuals, amounting to almost half of her small canon. I count two letters to women friends, five to her husband, Li Yi (Li Zian), and some fourteen, the largest group, to men who are, in various degrees, friends, fellow writers, and lovers (or potential lovers). When she writes to her husband, it is always to say how much she longs to be with him, and misses him. Her response to their separation is consistent and strong, and the authenticity of her emotion is unmistakable, suggesting that he was indeed the great love of her life.

She thus places herself among the sorrowful, separated wives whose situations, sympathetically represented by male poets, make for some of the most moving poems in the classical Chinese tradition. Such women had even, from time to time, been given a voice by the male poets who contemplated them—Li Bai's (Li Po's) "The River Merchant's Wife, A Letter," is the most famous such example. Here, though, is a woman giving her own voice to the poem of lament and absence. She can do so in her own person, and she can do so for others. That she can write about such women with exactitude and power—"Boudoir Resentment," "Early Autumn"—is scarcely surprising, given her own circumstances.

At the same time, Yu Xuanji is clearly not content with the simple role of the inconsolable wife, shut up at home and grieving for her husband's absence. The poems addressed to men testify to a rich emotional life, scarcely centered on a single individual. They tease, they commend, they revel in the remembered and anticipated pleasures of feasting, exchanging poems, meeting and parting, and making love. Addressed to a gallery of very different individuals, and with varying degrees of intimacy, they characterize and commemorate affairs and friendships, they flirt, they are tartly aware of distraction and fickleness, and they show warm admiration and affection where such emotions seem warranted.

The formal variety should be noted too. Many of the poets of this period find a favorite form—eight five-character lines, for example—and stick to it for every poem. Within this context, Yu Xuanji exhibits a certain restlessness. Her favorite choice is eight seven-character lines (used seventeen times), followed closely by eight five-character lines (twelve examples) and four seven-character lines (eleven examples). Then comes a scattering of unusual choices, used just once or twice—twelve five-character lines, twelve seven-character lines, eight six-character lines (all used twice), and poems of sixteen five-character lines and twenty-four seven-character lines (one each). The match of form to subject does not feel predictable. The four-line poems feel terse, of course, and the longer poems expansive, but both are used for the full range of her interest and attention.

We do not, as mentioned earlier, know the chronology to all this variety. Did Yu Xuanji turn from longing for her husband to consolation with other men? Did she move from multiple relationships into a concentration on one? Were all these experiences and emotions coterminous rather than sequential? And how much does literary convention dictate details and emotions that we are tempted to ascribe to biography and subjective emotion? There are no firm answers to such questions, but the ways in which they circulate around the poems help characterize the rich emotional world they convey.

Less tied to specific events or people are those poems that meditate on landscape, existence, human nature, and the poet's conflicting and resolving emotions. Her next largest category of poems, after those composed as letters, can be characterized as meditations centered on places. They combine, as so often in classical Chinese poetry, a prospect of scenery and history, time and space, with introspection and an urge to arrive at some kind of philosophical overview. I count some sixteen or seventeen poems that seem to belong to this category. They vary considerably in length and scope, in focus and tone, but quite often they conclude with a sense of the mixed quality of human life, its interpenetrating spheres of joy and sorrow, love and loss. The poems in this group, quite naturally, introduce us to the Daoist values the poet explored and embraced: a joyous understanding of the panorama of existence, in all its relativity and mystery, and a peace of mind achieved through meditation and enlarged perspectives, accepting what cannot be changed. Again, the human wisdom of these poems, as in "Living in the Mountains in the Summer," and "Curing Yourself When Lovesick," while it relies on received ideas of the time, feels remarkably authoritative in a writer so youthful. One feels that there were times when Yu Xuanji was able to come successfully to terms with her world, in all its intricacy and instability, and that she prized those moments for the way they could inform her poems and her life, in equal measures.

Chinese poetry works on parallelisms, which differ in significant ways from our concepts of the figurative, such as symbol, metaphor, simile, and metonymy. All these latter terms imply some kind of hierarchy, involving the literal, or "real," and the figurative, usually at one remove from direct experience and always in danger of being dismissed as rhetorical ornamentation. The likenesses, or rhymings, on which Chinese poetry is based—and much modern and postmodern poetry has taken its cues from this insight—dispense with hierarchy and with the literal/figurative distinction. Things are simply presented in a juxtaposed fashion so that our awareness may explore their similarities and differences. The literal and the figurative are always present, in a simultaneous fashion. Thus a mention of "willow" will invoke "parting" because of the custom of giving willow branches as a token of sorrow in farewell. The sexual properties and analogies connected to flowers are never entirely absent from their mention, but they are also never the sole point. In "Selling the Last Peonies," for example, the poet is obviously talking about beautiful young women, but it is just as clear that she is literally talking about her culture's prizing of this flower:

> who can afford these peonies?
> their price is much too high
>
> their arrogant aroma
> even intimidates butterflies
>
> flowers so deeply red
> they must have been grown in a palace
>
> leaves so darkly green
> dust scarcely dares to settle there ...

This is a rendering of four lines, treating each line as a free-verse couplet stanza in English. Each line/couplet is paired with its neighbor, and then the pairings are paired, so that the principle of juxtaposition spreads outward. First there is the implied link of peonies to desirable women, then the idea that high prices for them correspond to a perfume too strong even for butterflies, an insight that is next compared to the correlation/contrast of the blossoms' red color and the concentrated green of the leaves. Intensity of beauty and of being, almost to excess, is the organizing principle throughout. Meanwhile, the way of characterizing the color ("grown in a palace") glances backward to the idea of expensiveness and forward to the poem's teasing conclusion:

> if you wait till they're transplanted
> to the Imperial Gardens
>
> then you, young lords, will find
> you have no means to buy them.

We had "young lords of longing" at one point, but decided that the point was already well made in the rest of the poem. The poem's procedure is quite typical: the reader is invited to explore a number of parallels and possibilities without feeling too heavily constrained by the poem's "point" or "message." It is possible to simply admire the peonies, in their extravagance and beauty, and it is possible to feel that flowers that intimidate butterflies may tend dangerously toward the counterproductive. Creative response is required of us, and to read such an open and subtly constructed text is to explore and interpret for ourselves. The teasing tone, the wistful recognition that beauty of any kind is expensive, rare, and ephemeral, the complicit sympathy coupled with the note of mockery: all these are typical of Yu Xuanji's poetic voice and afforded by the principles of juxtaposition and parallelism that are integral parts of the poetic tradition within which she writes.

Besides parallelism, which presents an ever-interesting challenge to the translator, Chinese poems from the Tang offer a particular obstacle to successful rendering: their use of allusions—to other poems, to famous incidents and names from history and folklore, and to geography that is charged with associations built up by poetry, religious worship, and popular lore. The principle of parallelism is at work here too. Why not mention some famous character or incident while exploring parallels and letting the play of association establish a field of meaning for the reader to occupy? The problem, of course, for Western readers, is an absence of the cultural context that makes the allusions meaningful.

The answer, in some cases, is to detour around them. In others, a form of substitution may be effective. In addition, we have provided notes to the poems. They identify some of the more obscure allusions and thus clarify the places where we decided to keep proper names or culture-specific references. If to be a good reader of Chinese poetry requires creativity on a reader's part, it also requires a willingness to learn gradually about the civilization that produced such remarkable work.

I came to this project with a love for Chinese poetry and the experience of translating it that is chiefly represented in my collection, *Five T'ang Poets*. The project began as a collaboration with Tang Tao, a former Oberlin student, but she withdrew early on, and my partner in the enterprise became my friend and colleague, Jiann I. Lin, Oberlin's East Asian Librarian. His knowledge of the tradition and his patience in retrieving obscurities have been indispensable. He also provided the entire input of traditional Chinese characters, using a computer program to select characters that would be faithful to the classical texts.

As far as we know, no one has attempted to bring all of Yu Xuanji's poems together in English. Kenneth Rexroth included four of her poems in his *Women Poets of China* (1972). Other anthologies represent her even more briefly, if at all. There is an odd kind of biography, now forgotten. In 1936, Genevieve Wimsatt published a curious little volume, *Selling Wilted Peonies*, an attempt, necessarily conjectural and fictional, at reconstructing the poet's life. This "biography" contains versions of many of the poems; to say that they lack distinction as poems in English is to put the matter charitably. Nevertheless, Wimsatt's book, which was published by Columbia University Press, represents an early attempt to recognize this poet's importance.

Oberlin, Ohio   David Young
July 1997

The Clouds Float North

Poem for the Willows by the River

The calm blue sky and its reflection
frame the barren riverbanks

huge shapes of misty cloud
merge into distant mansions

upside-down, many images
spread on the autumn waters

flowers drop from time to time
onto the head of the fisherman

old roots mark the dens
where many fish are hiding

hanging branches offer mooring
to the boats of travelers

the night tosses and sighs
all filled with wind and rain

and dreaming astonishing dreams
only enlarges my gloom.

賦得江邊柳

翠色連荒岸	煙姿入遠樓	影鋪秋水面	花落釣人頭	根老藏魚窟
枝低繫客舟	蕭蕭風雨夜	驚夢復添愁		

Sent to a Neighbor Woman Friend

The sun admires us warmly
so we cover our arms with gauze silk sleeves

but the sad and fitful spring
makes us too lazy to put on makeup

it's easier to find
rare, unparalleled treasure

than it is to have and hold
one reliable lover

at night, against our pillows,
we weep our secret tears

by day, among the flowers,
we hide our breaking hearts

if we can have
great poets for friends

should we also long
for handsome lovers?

贈鄰女

羞日遮羅袖　　愁春嬾起妝　　易求無價寶　　難得有心郎　　枕上潛垂淚
花間暗斷腸　　自能窺宋玉　　何必恨王昌

The Fragrance of Orchids

The body that aches with longing
is drunk at dusk and again at dawn

these wild mutual yearnings
return to us each spring

there in the rain goes a messenger
bearing a passionate letter

under the open window
stands one with a broken heart

up in the mountains a lover
rolls up a pearl screen, looking out

sadness comes back and comes back
as fragrant and lush as the grass

and we're all walking home in the dark
from banquets and celebrations

or watching the quiet dust
that sifts down from our roof beams.

寄國香

旦夕醉吟身　　相思又此春　　雨中寄書使　　窗下斷腸人　　山捲珠簾看
愁隨芳草新　　別來清宴上　　幾度落梁塵

Tribute to a Master Alchemist

The gorgeous colored clouds
stitched into quilted robes

wonderful perfume coming
from a finely woven tapestry

the red hibiscus blooming
among its thick green leaves

mountains and water dressed
in a rare embroidered cape

—like stopping short in your tracks
to hear the song of a warbler

or freeing a crane from a cage
to watch it fly away

—sleeping alone on a spring night
in an old high-ceilinged chamber

or rain that arrives at dusk
falling thick and fast.

寄題鍊師

霞彩翦為衣　　添香出繡幃　　芙蓉花葉[ ]　　山水帔[ ]稀　　駐履聞鶯語
開籠放鶴飛　　高堂春睡覺　　暮雨正霏霏

Sent to Secretary Liu

I know you used to command
an army of veteran soldiers

marching them down new roads
as they chanted favorite ballads

forded Fenchuan River
in hard March rains

stood by Jinshui River in June
as flowers bloomed all around

but the vast sky gets locked away
behind its prison bars

and weapons of war, over time,
acquire a coat of dust—

now the scholar and the monk
can sit up late, admiring midnight

and visitors can linger
drunk and flushed on the lawn

the writing brush and inkstone
almost compose on their own

as poetry books form a circle
around the thoughtful self

and a modest talent for verse
begins to come to the surface

the way the orange carp rise
when you scatter food on their pond.

寄劉尚書

八座鎮雄軍	歌謠滿路新	汾川三月雨	晉水百花春	囹圄長空鎖
干戈久覆塵	儒僧觀子夜	羈客醉紅茵	筆硯行隨手	詩書坐繞身
小才多顧盼	得作食魚人			

Washing Yarn Temple

State plots against state
intrigues come thick and fast

but here at Washing Yarn Temple
Xi Shi offers us harmony

a pair of faces can beam
just from turning to glimpse her

while thousands of seasoned troops
ground their weapons and surrender

Fan Li achieved his greatness
by turning away from the world

while Wu Xu had to die
in order to wear down the government

the great river confers a name
upon a place like Zhuji

but this blue mountain has long been known
as a beautiful woman's birthplace.

浣紗廟

吳越相謀計策多　　浣紗神女已相和　　一雙笑靨縈迴面　　十萬精兵盡倒戈
范蠡功成身隱遯　　伍胥諫死國消磨　　只今諸暨長江畔　　空有青山號苧蘿

Selling the Last Peonies

Facing the wind makes us sigh
we know how many flowers fall

spring has come back again
and where have the fragrant longings gone?

who can afford these peonies?
their price is much too high

their arrogant aroma
even intimidates butterflies

flowers so deeply red
they must have been grown in a palace

leaves so darkly green
dust scarcely dares to settle there

if you wait till they're transplanted
to the Imperial Gardens

then you, young lords, will find
you have no means to buy them.

賣殘牡丹

臨風興歎落花頻　芳意潛消又一春　應為價高人不問　卻緣香甚蝶難親
紅英只稱生宮裡　翠葉那堪染路塵　及至移根上林苑　王孫方恨買無因

To Thank the Scholar Li for the Gift of a Bamboo Mat

This precious mat, newly spread out
in the Halcyon Pavilion

makes me think of the deep, clear water
that marks our local river

only a fan made of clouds
could match your priceless gift

I turn toward my silver bed
regretting the early autumn.

酬李學士寄簟

珍簟新鋪翡翠樓　　泓澄玉水記方流　　唯應雲扇情相似　　同向銀床恨早秋

Love Letter to Li Zian

I suck melting ice and munch cork bark
and still make no sense of my life

Jinshui River and Huguan Pass
keep coming up in my dreams

Qin Jing's mirror is ready to break
and I'm sad for the falling magpies

Emperor Shun's zither is tuned
and I blame the messenger swans

paulownia leaves by the well
cry in the autumn rain

the silver lamp by the window
dims in the wind at dawn

I write you letters across great distances
and never know if they reach you

holding a bamboo pole at sunset
next to a wide blue river.

情書寄李子安

飲冰食蘗志無功　　晉水壺關在夢中　　秦鏡欲分愁隨鵲　　舜琴將弄怨飛鴻
井邊桐葉鳴秋雨　　窗下銀燈暗曉風　　書信茫茫何處問　　持竿盡日碧江空

Boudoir Bitterness

The grass overgrown with weeds
fills her hands
as she weeps in the late sunlight

she's just heard
her neighbor's husband
has come back home

only the other day
wild swans and geese
were heading north

this morning they came again
honking and calling
migrating south

springs come
autumns go
heart-sorrow stays

autumns go
springs come
and still no news

she slides the bolts
of her red doors—
nobody's coming

why bother
pounding the laundry
or washing the curtains?

閨怨

靡蕪盈手泣斜暉　　聞道鄰家夫婿歸　　別日南鴻纔北去　　今朝北鴈又南飛
春來秋去相思在　　秋去春來信息稀　　扃閉朱門人不到　　砧聲何事透羅幃

Spring Thoughts Sent Affectionately to Zian

The mountain road is sheer
and the stone steps will be steep

I'll feel bitter twice—once for the journey,
and once for missing you

icy roads and empty ravines
will make me hear your voice

cool snow on distant peaks
will bring back your calm face

don't listen to popular songs
don't drink too much in spring

don't hobnob with idle drifters
don't spend whole nights playing chess

it's as though we shared a lovers' vow
one made of pine, not stone

it's as though we were paired lovebirds
whose rendezvous is delayed

we hate going on alone
trying to make it through winter

we may come back together
by the light of a great round moon

saying good-bye to you, my lord,
what keepsake can I offer?

eyes brimming and shining,
here's a poem just for you.

春情寄子安

山路欹斜石磴危　　不愁行苦苦相思　　冰銷遠澗憐清韻　　雪遠寒峰想玉姿
莫聽凡歌春病酒　　休招閑客夜貪棋　　如松匪石盟長在　　比翼連襟會宜遲
雖恨獨行冬盡日　　終期相見月圓時　　別君何物堪持贈　　淚落晴光一首詩

Watching Them Play Polo

Firm, round, clean and smooth,
the ball goes by like a comet

the crescent-shaped sticks crack sharply
nobody wants to stop

the riders, pulling free,
chase each other, jostling

I watch from behind the railing
staying as long as I like

around and around they go
the ball skipping just ahead of them

sometimes it seems as if
they'll never score a goal

but having begun their game
they ought to be able to finish it

and whoever plays the best
ought to be given a prize.

打毬作

堅圓淨滑一星流　　月杖爭敲未擬休　　無滯礙時從撥弄　　有遮攔處任鉤留
不辭宛轉長隨手　　卻恐相將不到頭　　畢竟入門應始了　　願君爭取最前籌

Sent to a Friend in a Late Spring Mood

The chatter of orioles
breaks up my dream

I put on a little makeup
to change my tear-stained face

a young moon
shines through the bamboo shade

the smooth river
fumes with late night mist

swallows are bringing mud in their beaks
to pack their nests

bees are gathering pollen
from open flowers

I alone feel yearning
without any limit

reciting my own poems
staring up through the pines.

暮春有感寄友人

鶯語驚殘夢　　輕妝改淚容　　竹陰初月薄　　江靜晚煙濃　　溪濕銜泥燕
香鬚採蕊蜂　　獨憐無限思　　吟罷亞枝松

Sent to Wen Feiqing on a Winter Night

I've racked my brains for a poem
chanting here by the lamp

spending a sleepless night
away from my chilly quilt

blown leaves fill the courtyard
the night wind makes me gloomy

through the cotton curtain and window screen
shines a deep and beautiful moon

we're distant and lack leisure time
to accomplish our mutual wishes

love rises and falls like a wave
and usually leaves our hearts helpless

a sparrow may live alone
unable to nest in a parasol tree

I heard one chirping at sunset
circling the woods in vain.

冬夜寄溫飛卿

苦思搜詩燈下吟　不眠長夜怕寒衾　滿庭木葉愁風起　透幌紗窗惜月沈
疏散未閑終遂願　盛衰空見本來心　幽棲莫定梧桐處　暮雀啾啾空繞林

A Poem Sent to Li Ying to Match His "Fishing in Summer"

It's odd that you and I live
here on the very same street

and not even once a year
do we run across each other

if you want to impress an old girl friend
you need to produce a pure poem

leaves of the fragrant cassia
break out along new boughs

the nature of the Tao
is simpler than ice or snow

the understanding of Zen
mocks the expense of gauze and silk

my spiritual footprints rise
into the empyrean

but there isn't any path
across love's waves and mist.

酬李郢夏日釣魚回見示

住處雖同巷　　經年不一過　　清詞勸舊女　　香桂折新柯　　道性欺冰雪
禪心笑綺羅　　跡登霄漢上　　無路接煙波

Matching Poem for My New Neighbor to the West, Inviting Him over for Wine

Imagine a small poem
chanted a hundred times

each word bringing new feelings
sounding golden

my thoughts have climbed the wall
between our houses

I gaze into the distance—
my heart's not made of stone

the Milky Way looks expectant
out there in the vastness

Hunan's rivers are waking up
the zither is fully tuned

every April the Cold Food Festival
leaves me a little homesick

silent night, mellow wine—
don't make me pour it alone.

次韻西鄰新居兼乞酒

一首詩來百度吟　新情字字又聲金　西看已有登垣意　遠望能無化石心
河漢期賒空極目　瀟湘夢斷罷調琴　況逢寒節添鄉思　寂夜佳醪莫獨斟

A Matching Poem, Reply to a Friend

Looking for ways to defeat the sadness
of staying at an inn

opening your love letter
admiring the elegant strokes

rain on Penglai Mountain
makes the thousand peaks look small

wind in the Xiegu Gorge
blows thousands of leaves into autumn

in the morning I read every word
looking down upon jasper

at night, curled in my quilt and bed
I read it all again

I should take out my sandalwood casket
and stow it safely away

but just for this moment, holding it,
I can't seem to let it go.

和友人次韻

何事能銷旅館愁　　紅牋開處見銀鉤　　蓬山雨灑千峰小　　嶰谷風吹萬葉秋
字字朝看輕碧玉　　篇篇夜誦在衿襠　　欲將香匣收藏卻　　且惜時吟在手頭

Two Poems

1. For the Successful Candidates of the Civil Service Exam

You can't stay long in wonderlands
or man-made worlds

it's as if you turn around
and find ten autumns gone

behind the curtain, under the quilt
an affectionate pair of mandarin ducks

here in the parrot's cage
the talking hasn't stopped

dew-streaked flowers, early morning
tell you of sorrowful faces

willows bending in evening wind
bring back pensive eyebrows

rosy clouds leave
they never come back

but Pan Yue's in love and willing to wait
until his hair turns white.

2. Grief for a Death

A laurel branch against the moon
matches the elegant mists

ten thousand peach trees by the river
stand in the rain, blooming red

if someone sets wine before you
you don't act disappointed

from ancient days to the present
sorrow and joy are twins.

和新及第悼亡詩二首

（1）
仙籍人間不久留　　片時已過十經秋　　鴛鴦帳下香猶暖　　鸚鵡籠中語未休
朝露綴花如臉恨　　晚風敧柳似眉愁　　彩雲一去無消息　　潘岳多情欲白頭

（2）
一枝月桂和煙秀　　萬樹江桃帶雨紅　　且醉尊前休悵望　　古來悲樂與今同

Visiting the South Pavilion at Chongzhen Temple Where the Civil Service Exam Results Are Posted

Cloudy mountains fill my gaze—
I think they enjoy the spring

under skillful fingers
great calligraphy is born

I wish my woman's clothing
didn't obscure my poems

raising my head in vain
admiring the names on the honor rolls.

遊崇真觀南樓睹新及第題名處

雲峰滿目放春晴　　歷歷銀鉤指下生　　自恨羅衣掩詩句　　舉頭空羨榜中名

Melancholy Thoughts

Leaves falling one by one
and rain at dusk is tender

vermilion lute, playing alone
sound of a clear voice singing

try to ignore your regret
at having no intimate friends or lovers

try to build up your character
and cast your bitterness into the sea

sound of a carriage outside the door
come for some venerable elder

heaps of Taoist books
scattered in front of the pillow

raggedly dressed people
eventually go to heaven

green water and blue hills
already here and gone.

愁思

落葉紛紛暮雨和　　朱絲獨撫自清歌　　放情休恨無心友　　養性空拋苦海波
長者車音門外有　　道家書卷枕前多　　布衣終作雲霄客　　綠水青山時一過

Autumn Lament

You sigh, you're full of tenderness,
it's more than you can bear

too many love affairs, too much wind and moon—
and the courtyard is loaded with autumn

the sound of the water-clock's close by—
just outside your bridal chamber

and night by night, next to the lamp,
your hair is turning white.

秋怨

自歎多情是足愁　　汎當風月滿庭秋　　洞房偏與更聲近　　夜夜燈前欲白頭

River Journey

We cross the Yangtze diagonally
heading for Wuchang city

passing Parrot Island
where thousands of families live

in the early hours the painted barge
has a cargo of lovers and sleepers

and I dream I've become a butterfly
seeking the flowers too

•

Dim mist and we're already sailing
into Cormorant Harbor

I thought we were still in the middle
somewhere near Parrot Island

I went to bed drunk, lay awake
singing all kinds of nonsense

got up on the Hanjiang River side
stunned to be back on dry land.

江行

（1）
大江橫抱武昌斜　　鸚鵡洲前戶萬家　　畫舸春眠朝未足　　夢為蝴蝶也尋花

（2）
煙花已入鸕鶿港　　畫舸猶沿鸚鵡洲　　醉臥醒吟都不覺　　今朝驚在漢江頭

Hearing Squire Li Had Gone Fishing, I Sent Him This Poem

No limit to the lotuses' fragrance
they match the color of your summer clothes

my darling, don't pole your boat
into places you can't get back from

I wish we could match the affection
of all those mandarin ducks

swimming around in pairs
close by your fishing rock.

聞李端公垂釣回寄贈

無限荷香染暑衣　　阮郎何處弄船歸　　自慚不及鴛鴦侶　　猶得雙雙近釣磯

The Zifu Temple, Founded by the Hermit Ren

Someone who liked seclusion
built this marvelous place

now sightseers and tourists
can stop and rest awhile

they write their words in vain
upon the white-washed walls

in the palace of the lotus
their names cannot be found

the pond is dug in such a way
that the spring flows naturally

the path is made so well
that grass grows lush beside it

the Golden Wheel Pavilion
is hundreds of feet high

and it faces the river—
clear, eye-catching, bright.

題任處士刱資福寺

幽人刱奇境　　遊客駐行程　　粉壁空留字　　蓮宮未有名　　鑿池泉自出
開徑草重生　　百尺金輪閣　　當川豁眼明

The Yinwu Pavilion

Blossoms of spring, the autumn moon—
you have to turn them into poems

the bright days, the clear nights—
you feel surrounded by floating gods

I rolled up the curtain idly
and never rolled it back

I moved my couch to face the mountains
and slept here from then on.

題隱霧亭

春花秋月入詩篇　　白日清霄是散仙　　空捲珠簾不曾下　　長移一榻對山眠

The Double Ninth Festival Delayed by Rain

The courtyard is full of yellow chrysanthemums
all broken and drooping along the hedge

two flowers, hibiscus and image,
gape at each other's reflections

I put my hat back on the table—
no going out in this wind and rain

and I'm too tipsy to recall
where I put down my golden cup.

重陽阻雨

滿庭黃菊籬邊拆　　兩朵芙蓉鏡裡開　　落帽臺前風雨阻　　不知何處醉金杯

Early Autumn

Pastel chrysanthemum buds
shine like newly dyed silk

distant mountains
lounge in the sunset mist

a cool wind stirs
the great green trees

a clear song throbs
in the vermilion lute

pining for her husband
she spins to make brocade

he's stationed beyond the Great Wall,
under the open sky

wild geese, fly there fast
fish, go through the waters

they need your comings and goings
to carry precious letters.

早秋

| 嫩菊含新彩 | 遠山閑夕煙 | 涼風驚綠樹 | 清韻入朱弦 | 思婦機中錦 |
| 征人塞外天 | 鴈飛魚在水 | 書信若為傳 | | |

Remembering Strong Emotions

I find myself full of hate
for this vermilion lute

when I know perfectly well
how much I ought to love it

remembering clouds and rain
— our passionate affair

I shouldn't be stirring up
those lost perfumes

gifted disciples—
brilliant plums and peaches

nothing should hurt the career
of such an eminent scholar

dark green pines
vast and hazy laurels

admiration coming in
from people all over the world

the moonlight colors the moss
on the clear steps of the terrace

sound of a voice that's singing
deep in a bamboo courtyard

red leaves all over the ground
and heaped against the door

not to be cleared away
until *he* comes to visit.

感懷寄人

恨寄朱弦上　含情意不任　早知雲雨會　未起蕙蘭心　灼灼桃兼李
無妨國士尋　蒼蒼松與桂　仍羨世人欽　月色苔階淨　歌聲竹院深
門前紅葉地　不埽待知音

For a Friend Who Didn't Arrive Because of Heavy Rain

The wild geese and fish, those messengers,
have carried mail in vain

the rooster and the broom corn
are sad that we didn't meet

I close the door and sigh
caught in a cage of moonlight

I lift the curtain and find its silk
already coming to pieces

close by, spring water whistles
crowding its stone channel

farther away, muddy waves
lap at the river's banks

homesickness strikes travelers
out on the road in autumn

me, I recite an old poem—
five characters to the line.

期友人阻雨不至

鴈魚空有信　　雞黍恨無期　　閉戶方籠月　　褰簾已散絲　　近泉鳴砌畔
遠浪漲江渚　　鄉思悲秋客　　愁吟五字詩

Visiting Master Zhao and Not Finding Him

I wanted to be with someone
of spiritual refinement

I find his house is empty,
only the maid is home

his crucible's still warm
from cooking up herb medicines

outside in the courtyard
tea leaves are still simmering

a few dim lamps
next to the painted walls

a long shadow by the signal pole
that faces the setting sun

as I leave I keep turning around
hoping to find he's come back—

just a few blooming branches
brushing the outside walls.

訪趙鍊師不遇

何處同仙侶　　青衣獨在家　　暖爐留煮藥　　鄰院為煎茶　　畫壁燈光暗
幡竿日影斜　　殷勤重回首　　牆外數枝花

Curing Yourself When Lovesick

You're free and at leisure now
no company to distract you

you can travel by yourself
to see great sights and views

clouds part—there's the river
and the bright moon overhead

loosen the mooring rope
and let your boat go drifting

play your lute
in old Liang dynasty temples

recite your poems
in Yu Liang's garden pavilions

take bamboo groves
for boon companions

make friends with rocks
in steep outcroppings

and let your whole wealth be
ordinary swallows and sparrows

forget about gold and silver
forget about ambition

spring will fill your cup
with good green wine

moon will come silently by night
to visit at your window

walk around the pond
watch it clear and settle

take out your hairpin
by your reflection in the stream

and lie there in your bed
with books spread all around you

a little too happy to bother
rising to fix your hair.

遣懷

閑散身無事　　風光獨自遊　　斷雲江上月　　解纜海中舟　　琴弄蕭梁寺
詩吟庾亮樓　　叢篁堪作伴　　片石好為儔　　燕雀徒為貴　　金銀志不求
滿杯春酒綠　　對月夜窗幽　　繞砌澄清沼　　抽簪映細流　　臥床書冊遍
半醉起梳頭

Sent to Feiqing

Crickets chirp on the stair-steps
they sound confused to me

in the misty courtyard, along the branches,
clear dewdrops hang

a moonlit night—I hear faint music
coming from my neighbor's

if I went upstairs I could see the mountains
distinct even in the distance

a cool breeze comes to stroke me
as I sit on my bamboo mat

and I wish I had a magic lute
to help me get through this life

I feel like that philosopher
who wrote such lazy letters

wanting some way to express
the moods and thoughts of autumn.

寄飛卿

階砌亂蛩鳴　　庭柯煙露清　　月中鄰樂響　　樓上遠山明　　珍簟涼風著
瑤琴寄恨生　　嵇君嬾書札　　底物慰秋情

Visiting Ezhou

Willows get in the way, orchids are grotesque,
blossoms smother their branches

below Stone City's walls the boats
sail slowly through the dusk

what's on top of Zhepai mountain?
the ancient poet Qu Yuan's grave

what's on Yuanhuo peak?
the flags of the magistrate's carriage

white snow makes a high, thin music
writing its poems on old temples

sunlit spring is a new poem
set to a brilliant melody

don't be sad that a soul
fords the clear river and is gone—

that's what makes travelers compose
ten thousand poems in vain.

過鄂州

柳拂蘭撓花滿枝　　石城城下暮帆遲　　折牌峰上三閭墓　　遠火山頭五馬旗
白雪調高題舊寺　　陽春歌在換新詞　　莫愁魂逐清江去　　空使行人萬首詩

Living in the Mountains in Summer

I've moved and now I live up here
where gods could make their homes

the shrubs and thickets mix and bloom—
nobody had to plant them

the little tree in the courtyard
is where I hang my laundry

all the wine I can drink
from this mountain spring I sit by

my windows and my hallways
go deep through the bamboo trail

I use my silky clothes
to wrap up heaps of scattered books

rowing out idly in my decorated boat
chanting poems to the radiant moon

and the light breeze blows and blows—
I can trust it to bring me back.

夏日山居

移得仙居此地來　　花叢自遍不曾栽　　庭前亞樹張衣桁　　坐上新泉泛酒杯
軒檻暗傳深竹徑　　綺羅長擁亂書堆　　閑乘畫舫吟明月　　信任輕風吹卻回

Late Spring Improvisation

Very few visitors or lovers
come through this alley to this hidden door

and as for someone I can really cherish
I meet him only in dreams

perfumed gauze and damask—
whose empty seat at the banquet?

songs carried on the wind—
coming from what pavilion?

around here it's mostly army drums
disrupting morning sleep

nothing but magpies in the courtyard
chattering through spring sorrow

how could I hope to have any part
in the world of grand events

my own life at such a distance
and no place to tie up my boat?

暮春即事

深巷窮門少侶儔　阮郎唯有夢中留　香飄羅綺誰家席　風送歌聲何處樓
街近鼓鼙喧曉睡　庭閑鵲語亂春愁　安能追逐人間事　萬里身同不繫舟

Joining Somebody's Mourning

You've seen her, bloom of the peach,
posture graceful as jade

breeze through willows and poplars
delicate arch of the eyebrows

pearl hoard in a dragon's cave
that shock of recognition

glimpsed in the mirror at state functions
happy among the chitchat

now changed to a somber dream
lost in mist on a rainy night

hating to hear the story
of bitter times and solitude

hills to the west, sunset
hills to the east, moonrise

and thoughts of loss
that are never going to end.

代人悼亡

曾睹夭桃想玉姿　帶風楊柳認蛾眉　珠歸龍窟知誰見　鏡在鸞臺話向誰
從此夢悲煙雨夜　不堪吟苦寂寥時　西山日落東山月　恨想無因有了期

Letter to a Friend

Both busy streets and country roads
are empty without good friends

evenings go, mornings come,
and I pawn my embroidered dress

the dusky mirror, frail in its special box,
shows me my delicate hair, tangled across my face

my incense burner, curiously carved,
creates a haze of musky smoke

lovesick with spring, wealthy young men
leave me urgent messages

sometimes I think of famous beauties
their portraits in the doorways

lovers' chariots don't spare
to line up at my door

willows bend thoughtfully and plum blossoms burst
rich with fragrance, just in time.

和人

茫茫九陌無知己　　暮去朝來典繡衣　　寶匣鏡昏蟬鬢亂　　博山爐暖麝煙微
多情公子春留句　　少思文君畫掩扉　　莫惜羊車頻列載　　柳絲梅綻正芳菲

Sent to Zian, Long Distance, from the Hanjiang River

Gazing across at each other, helpless,
from the north and south banks of this river

frustrated, speaking each other's poems,
recalling our times together

—that pair of mandarin ducks looks happy
swimming warmly next to the sandbar

and those two teals are without a care
as they fly through the tangerine grove

I hear a faint sound of singing now
rising up with the chimney smoke

I watch the deep and brilliant moonlight
next to the empty ferry slip

even if we were a few feet apart
my feelings would have to cross miles

listening sadly as they pound laundry
in distant family compounds.

隔漢江寄子安

江南江北愁望　　相思相憶空吟　　鴛鴦暖臥沙浦　　鸂鶒閑飛橘林
煙裡歌聲隱隱　　渡頭月色沈沈　　含清咫尺千里　　況聽家家遠砧

An Allegory

Peach blossoms everywhere, pink
color of spring

silver willows by every house
moon-bright

someone upstairs, trying on new clothes
waiting for nightfall

somebody else, alone in her bedroom
drowning in tenderness

the carp play around with the lotuses
under the moon

the sparrows call out to the rainbow
at the horizon

joys and sorrows, these are the dreams
we have in this world

why do they always come to us
in pairs?

寓言

紅桃處處春色　　碧柳家家月明　　樓上新妝待夜　　閨中獨坐含情
芙蓉月下魚戲　　蟪蛛天邊雀聲　　人世悲歡一夢　　如何得作雙成

Letter to Zian, Sad from Gazing into the Distance, from Jiangling

The maple leaves on their trees
branch after branch

at sunset the river bridge
frames the returning boats

oh my lord this longing for you
is like the water in West River

flowing east all day, all night
never a moment of rest.

江陵愁望寄子安

楓葉千枝復萬枝　　江橋掩映暮帆遲　　憶君心似西江水　　日夜東流無歇時

Sent to Zian

Someone is drunk, but a thousand wine-pots
can't wash off the melancholy

somebody wants a way to untie
a hundred sad knots of separation

the orchids go off for a little rest
in spring they return to the gardens

and willows growing to the east and west
entangle the boats of travelers

sadness of being together, sadness of parting,
the clouds keep changing their shapes

love and affection should be like the river
whose current never stops

in the season of blossoms it's hard
to find an intimate lover

who wants to get drunk all alone
sitting up here in Jade Tower?

寄子安

醉別千巵不浣愁　　離腸百結解無由　　蕙蘭銷歇歸春圃　　楊柳東西絆客舟
聚散已悲雲不定　　恩情須學水長流　　有花時節知難遇　　未宜厭厭醉玉樓

Saying Goodbye

Several nights in this gorgeous pavilion
and I began to have expectations

until my darling surprised me—
he had to be off on a journey

so I sleep alone and don't discuss
the whereabouts of clouds

around the lamp, now almost spent,
one lost moth is circling.

送別

秦樓幾夜愜心期　　不料仙郎有別離　　睡覺莫言雲去處　　殘燈一颭野蛾飛

A Warm Note to Squire Li Jinren

Today I'm happy, hearing
the chatter of the magpies

last night in the lamplight
both of us burned the candle

lighting some incense I step outside
to greet my handsome guest

I don't even envy that happy couple
the Weaver Girl and the Cowherd.

迎李近仁員外

今日喜時聞喜鵲　　昨宵燈下拜燈花　　焚香出戶迎潘岳　　不羨牽牛織女家

Saying Goodbye, II

Softly the water chases itself,
knowing it's hard to be settled and certain

clouds arrive without any plan
and we wish we could call them back

a desolate spring breeze,
the Yangtze stretched out in the twilight

and a mandarin duck, swimming alone—
its flock already gone.

送別

水柔逐器知難定　　雲出無心宜再歸　　惆悵春風楚江暮　　鴛鴦一隻失群飛

Letter to an Exam Candidate, from Shanxi to the Capital

I've stayed at home here, idle,
mostly composing poems
for several sorrowful years

gazing out toward
the Wangwu Mountains
site of our old excursions

reciting my verses, facing
east, facing west, mixed up—
a mountain range with a thousand peaks

or a horse that wanders south
and then heads north
whichever way the brook flows—

remembering rainy nights
we two spent together
feasting

and then, after saying goodbye
in the blossom season,
climbing the stairs alone

and the sudden knock on the door
—oh happy little door—
announcing your arrival

and the quiet lane
where our secluded house
was set apart for love . . .

Xiangru's lute has stopped
its red strings
snapped

a pair of nesting swallows
separate
in the white dew of autumn

don't forget about
your rural friend—
visit once in a while!

every spring there's busy traffic
here in the Yangtze Delta—
you can catch a ride!

左名場自澤州至京使人傳語

閑居作賦幾年愁　王屋山前是舊遊　詩詠東西千嶂亂　馬隨南北一泉流
曾陪雨夜同歡席　別後花時獨上樓　忽喜扣門傳語至　為憐鄰巷小房幽
相如琴罷朱弦斷　雙燕巢分白露秋　莫倦蓬門時一訪　每春忙在曲江頭

Reply to a Poem, Matching the Form

The blood-red bustle, the purple muddle
of this human world . . .

alone and quiet, chanting,
in the midst of sunlit scenery

giving up wanting a lover
or hoping for literary fame

conceiving a wonderful poem
in the midst of a fortified village

plain flowers, so simple and right
I'm ashamed to express my gratitude

residing secluded, in a back lane,
becoming a sage like Yan Yuan

so full of affection there's no need
to long for company all the time

just as pines and other such plants are content
simply to live among mountains.

和人次韻

喧喧朱紫雜人寰　　獨自清吟日色間　　何事玉郎搜藻思　　忽將瓊韻扣柴關
白花發詠慚稱謝　　僻巷深居謬學顏　　不用多情欲相見　　松蘿高處是前山

Three Beautiful Sisters, Orphaned Young

We used to hear about the south,
its splendid fresh appearance

now it's these eastern neighbors
these sisters three

up in the loft, inspecting their trousseaus
reciting a verse about parrots

sitting by blue-green windows
embroidering phoenix garments

their courtyard filled with colorful petals
like red smoke, billowing unevenly

their cups full of good green wine
tasted one by one

•

It's dreadful, staring into the mystic pond,
knowing you'll always be female

banished from heaven, stuck in this life,
unable to do what men do

a poet who happens to have some beauty,
ends up being compared

to a gorgeous woman who's silent—
that makes me feel ashamed

me, singing solo love songs
upon this vanishing zither

plucking the four strings softly
murmuring the words

facing my mirror and dressing table
to admire my black silk hair

as if I could rival the moon
by flaunting a white jade hairpin

•

A little cave among the pines
where dew drips down

the sky above the willows
a great net filled with mist

when you can be like the rain
your heart will have strength to go on

and you won't be afraid to blow the flute
before you've fully mastered it

my mother would get upset
because I talked to flowers

and my lover was from the past
a poet who came to me in dreams

•

The spirit makes fine, fresh verses
and then is broken

it's like watching a lovely young woman
give up her will to live

these gorgeous young creatures
who knows what they'll come to?

the clouds float north
the clouds float south.

光威裒姊妹三人, 少孤而始妍, 乃有是作, 精粹難儔, 雖
謝家聯[ ], 何以加之, 有客自京師來者示予, 因次其韻

碧窗應繡鳳凰衫　妝閣相看鸚鵡賦　今日東鄰姊妹三　昔聞南國容華少
謫來塵世未為男　恐向瑤池曾作女　綠醑盈杯次第銜　紅芳滿院參差折
四弦輕撥語喃喃　一曲豔歌琴杳杳　西子無言我更慚　文姬有貌終堪比
大羅天上柳煙含　小有洞中松露滴　對月爭誇白玉簪　當臺競鬥青絲髮
潘郎曾向夢中參　阿母幾嗔花下語　不怕吹簫事未諳　但能為雨心長在
行雲歸北又歸南　悵望佳人何處在　若睹紅顏死亦甘　暫持清句魂猶斷

Snapping Willows

Saying goodbye, morning after morning,
weeping, wearing flower jewelry

picking misty willow wands
in strong spring breeze

I wish West Hill
were bare of trees

I keep thinking that would help
to stop these falling tears.

折楊柳

朝朝送別泣花鈿　　折盡春風楊柳煙　　願得西山無樹木　　免教人作淚懸懸

Fragments

1

Burning incense
climbs the jade altar

I hold an invitation
to a golden palace ceremony.

2

Brilliant moonlight
shining in a hidden clearing

crisp wind blows open
the front of a short gown.

3

Gorgeous fields along the road
a deep springtime vista

beautiful emblem of the season
source of my playful mood.

4

Pleading,
unable to speak

red tears, first one, then
a pair, traveling down.

5

The high cloud loves itself
so why these gloomy common dreams?

the heavenly look lasts ...
again that fragrance, better than flowers.

句

焚香登玉壇　　端簡禮金闕

明月照幽隙　　清風開短襟

綺陌春望遠　　瑤徽春興多

殷勤不得語　　紅淚一雙流

雲情自鬱爭同夢　　仙貌長芳又勝花

NOTES

We have used the order of Yu Xuanji's poems as anthologized in *Quan Tang Shi*, which includes 2,200 poets of the Tang Dynasty (618–907). The edition we used is the 1967 Taipei reprint based on the 1662 (Kangxi era) woodblock print edition. All Chinese names and titles are romanized in "Chinese pinyin."

There is no way to know whether the order of her poems in the anthology is chronological, early to late, but that seems the best guess, since the poems are not grouped by subject or form. For each poem, we give a note on the form, along with romanizations in Chinese pinyin of the title and first line.

"Poem for the Willows by the River" (p. 1)
 Eight five-character lines in the original.
 Title: *Fu de jiang bian liu*
 First line: *Cui se lian huang an*

Willows were a correlative for sorrow at parting (see note to "Snapping Willows," p. 57). A conventional subject like this was a test of the poet's gift at improvised response on a familiar theme.

"Sent to a Neighbor Woman Friend" (p. 2)
 Eight five-character lines.
 Title: *Zeng lin nü*
 First line: *Xiu ri zhe luo xiu*

Yu Xuanji is in fact specific about the "great poets" and "handsome lovers" of the closing lines. She mentions Song Yu, a third century B.C. poet, and Wang Chang, a Tang Dynasty government official known for his good looks.

"The Fragrance of Orchids" (p. 3)
> Eight five-character lines.
> Title: *Ji guo xiang*
> First line: *Dan xi zui yin shen*

A poem that shows this poet's imaginative range and philosophical tendency. The final two images are particularly original. The title does not actually mention orchids. It uses the phrase *guo xiang*, which translates as "top fragrance in the nation." That is, as everyone would have understood, the orchid. Similar epithets, such as "top color" (peony), have been around a long time and are still in use.

"Tribute to a Master Alchemist" (p. 4)
> Eight five-character lines.
> Title: *Ji ti lian shi*
> First line: *Xia cai jian wei yi*

A character is missing from the third line (fifth character) and another (fourth character) from the fourth. Interest in alchemy was a significant feature of Daoism in Yu Xuanji's time.

"Sent to Secretary Liu" (p. 5)
> Twelve five-character lines.
> Title: *Ji Liu shang shu*
> First line: *Ba zuo zhen xiong jun*

The official in question had a title, *shang shu,* which could be translated as "Minister." The poem opens by invoking the sedan chair, carried by a crew of eight, that symbolized his importance. The poem may remark on his different life in peacetime, or commemorate his retirement from official duties. The scholar and monk referred to in the seventh couplet are Confucian and Buddhist, respectively. This portrait complements that of the alchemist, in no. 4, but is less idealized.

"Washing Yarn Temple" (p. 7)
  Eight seven-character lines.
  Title: *Huan sha miao*
  First line: *Wu Yue xiang mou ji ce duo.*

This was a temple dedicated to the famous beauty, Xi Shi, of the fifth century B.C. The poem is full of specific allusions: to the warring states of Wu and Yue, in the first line; to Fan Li, Xi Shi's husband, in the fifth and eighth lines; to Wu Xu (or Wu Zixu), of the same era (d. 484 B.C.), in the sixth line; to Zhuji County of Zhejiang Province, near the Yangtze (Changjiang) Delta, in the seventh line; and to the mountain known as Zhuluo, Xi Shi's birthplace, in the eighth line. In general the poem seems to celebrate her greatness, along with her husband, as existing outside the circles of power struggle and court intrigue and being therefore the more notable over time.

"Selling the Last Peonies" (p. 8)
  Eight seven-character lines.
  Title: *Mai can mu dan*
  First line: *Lin feng xing tan luo hua pin*

Discussed briefly in the Introduction. This, along with "Letter to Zian . . . from Jiangling," p. 46, is one of Yu Xuanji's best-known poems. Peonies had familiar associations with Chinese emperors. Beautiful young women sometimes disappeared into the Imperial Compound, out of the reach of their young admirers.

"To Thank the Scholar Li for the Gift of a Bamboo Mat" (p. 9)
  Four seven-character lines.
  Title: *Chou Li xue shi ji dian*
  First line: *Zhen dian xin pu fei cui lou*

Li was a very common name in this period, and it is difficult to know whether the "Li" of this poem is identical to the recipients named Li of other poems in Yu Xuanji's canon. Li was also the family name of the ruling dynasty, and because it could be connected to the founder of Daoism, Laozi (Lao-tzu), the supposed link helped make Daoism the religion most favored by the state in this period.

"Love Letter to Li Zian" (p. 10)
   Eight seven-character lines.
   Title: *Qing shu ji Li Zi an*
   First line: *Yin bing shi bo zhi wu gong*

The first (in order of arrangement in the anthology) of several letter poems addressing her husband after their separation. Again, specific allusions to particular places and to historical personages are plentiful. The mirror of polished bronze was something the magistrate had on the wall behind his official seat of judgment, to symbolize his integrity and clarity of judgment. The tuned zither of the long-ago emperor suggested a rare harmony of social forces and personal issues. These allusions take their place in the poet's inventory of melancholy responses to her world.

"Boudoir Bitterness" (p. 11)
   Eight seven-character lines.
   Title: *Gui yuan*
   First line: *Mi wu ying shou qi xie hui*

The two characters that make up the title were often used to characterize the unhappiness of women who had to stay home while their husbands traveled on official business or enjoyed the relative freedom of males in a patriarchal society. They weren't literally alone, in most cases, but their misery is usually made more poignant by depicting them in solitude. Many of the images—the overgrown grass, the migrating geese, the bolted gates or doors, the home that is getting neglected and unkempt—are typical of this subgenre.

"Spring Thoughts Sent Affectionately to Zian" (p. 13)
   Twelve seven-character lines.
   Title: *Chun qing ji Zi an*
   First line: *Shan lu qi xie shi deng wei*

Here the perspective is that of the wife left behind. The affirmation of love, despite separation, is the main point in either case.

"Watching Them Play Polo" (p. 15)
    Eight seven-character lines.
    Title: *Da qiu zuo*
    First line: *Jian yuan jing hua yi xing liu*

This poem reflects the fashion of its time for a game very much like polo. Whether Yu Xuanji intends any analogies to other male activities (i.e., literature), where she is also sidelined as a spectator, is conjectural.

"Sent to a Friend in a Late Spring Mood" (p. 16)
    Eight five-character lines.
    Title: *Mu chun you gan ji you ren*
    First line: *Ying yu jing can meng*

A kind of objective self-portrait.

"Sent to Wen Feiqing on a Winter Night" (p. 17)
    Eight seven-character lines.
    Title: *Dong ye ji Wen Fei qing*
    First line: *Ku si sou shi deng xia yin*

This is addressed to one of the best and most famous poets of the period, whose real name is Wen Tingyun, ca. 812 to ca. 870. While it somewhat resembles a love poem, it seems more to be a communication from one poet to another.

"A Poem Sent to Li Ying to Match His 'Fishing in Summer'" (p. 18)
    Eight five-character lines.
    Title: *Chou Li Ying xia ri diao yu hui jian shi*
    First line: *Zhu chu sui tong xiang*

This and the following two poems achieve an exceptional tonal complexity as they combine literary exchange (and rivalry) with flirtation, friendship, and some rueful self-mockery.

"Matching Poem for My New Neighbor to the West, Inviting Him over for Wine"
(p. 19)
> Eight seven-character lines.
> Title: *Ci yun xi lin xin ju jian qi jiu*
> First line: *Yi shou shi lai bai du yin*

> The Hunan rivers are two, Xiao and Xiang. The Cold Food Festival is in early
> April.

"A Matching Poem, Reply to a Friend" (p. 20)
> Eight seven-character lines.
> Title: *He you ren ci yun*
> First line: *He shi neng xiao lü guan chou*

> We have retained the specific place names. Penglai Mountain was a mythical
> place in the Eastern Sea; Xiegu Gorge was in the Kunlun Mountains, far to the
> west. The sense is of an expanse, with the imagination seeing as far as it can in
> both directions.

"Two Poems" (p. 21)
> The first of these is eight seven-character lines, the second four seven-character
> lines.
> Titles: *He xin ji di*
>   *Dao wang shi er shou*
> First lines: *Xian ji ren jian bu jiu liu*
>   *Yi zhi yue gui he yan xiu*

> The civil service exams (also called Imperial exams) allow candidates to qualify
> for various bureaucratic positions, from the lowest to the highest. The ability to
> compose poems on assigned topics was the significant mark of success. Since
> successful exam candidates had to be men, Yu Xuanji felt her exclusion keenly.
>   While their juxtaposition seems odd, these poems have in common a
> philosophical perspective and an urge to give advice. In the first, success is seen
> as temporary and to some extent illusory. The men are perhaps warned not to
> forget love and relationships with women as they climb the ladder of success. In
> the second, the simultaneous presence of loss and beauty in the world is empha-
> sized.
>   Pan Yue was a handsome poet of the Western Jin Dynasty (265-316).

"Visiting the South Pavilion at Chongzhen Temple Where the Civil Service Exam Results Are Posted" (p. 23)

Four seven-character lines.

Title: *You Chongzhen guan nan lou du xin ji di ti ming chu*

First line: *Yun feng man mu fang chun qing*

This is the poem in which Yu Xuanji is most explicit about her sense of disadvantage in combining literary talent with female gender.

"Melancholy Thoughts" (p. 24)

Eight seven-character lines.

Title: *Chou si*

First line: *Luo ye fen fen mu yu he*

In some ways, this seems a continuation of the previous poem, as though the poet were giving herself advice on how to cope with her problematic situation.

"Autumn Lament" (p. 25)

Four seven-character lines.

Title: *Qiu yuan*

First line: *Zi tan duo qing shi zu chou*

Here the note of melancholy is countered with rueful humor and a kind of teasing of the human tendency to self-pity.

"River Journey" (p. 26)

Eight seven-character lines (in two parts, but not marked as two separate poems.

Title: *Jiang xing*

First line: *Da jiang heng bao Wu chang xie*

This poem about crossing the Yangtze (Changjiang) River to Wuchang, part of Wuhan city in Hubei Province, turns philosophical as it invokes the dream of the butterfly, recalling the philosopher Zhuangzi (Chuang-tzu), who developed a sense of relativity and the instability of reality (was he a philosopher who dreamed he was a butterfly or a butterfly dreaming he was a philosopher?) from such a dream. There is also a popular folk tale about two lovers separated by death who reunite by turning into butterflies. The boat's motion joins the intoxication as metaphoric representation of the poet's state of inspiration.

"Hearing Squire Li Had Gone Fishing, I Sent Him This Poem" (p. 27)
  Four seven-character lines.
  Title: *Wen Li Duan gong chui diao hui ji zeng*
  First line: *Wu xian he xiang ran shu yi*

Another poem of affectionate rivalry and flirtation. We have used "Squire" to match the sense of a country gentleman, a man of moderate importance.

"The Zifu Temple, Founded by the Hermit Ren" (p. 28)
  Eight five-character lines.
  Title: *Ti Ren chu shi chuang Zi fu si*
  First line: *You ren chuang qi jing*

The characters of the temple's name, *Zi* and *fu*, mean "Good Fortune."

"The Yinwu Pavilion" (p. 29)
  Four seven-character lines.
  Title: *Ti Yin wu ting*
  First line: *Chun hua qiu yue ru shi pian*

The characters of the pavilion's name mean "Hidden Fog" or "Shaded Mist." This poem can be compared to "Living in the Mountains in Summer," p. 40, celebrating rural peace and retreat from the busy world.

"The Double Ninth Festival Delayed by Rain" (p. 30)
  Four seven-character lines.
  Title: *Chong yang zu yu*
  First line: *Man ting huang ju li bian chai*

The festival referred to is called Chongyang, on the ninth day of the ninth month in the Chinese lunar calendar. The season is roughly equivalent to mid-October.

"Early Autumn" (p. 31)
    Eight five-character lines.
    Title: *Zao qiu*
    First line: *Nen ju han xin cai*

Another poem of a separated couple. The husband, in the army, is involved in fighting beyond the borders of the empire. Wild geese and fish were supposed to help carry messages.

"Remembering Strong Emotions" (p. 32)
    Twelve five-character lines.
    Title: *Gan huai ji ren*
    First line: *Hen ji zhu xian shang*

It seems likely that this is a poem about Li Zian, the husband from whom Yu Xuanji was separated. The middle section, which speaks with admiration about his fame and achievement, also has a slightly sardonic feel.

"For a Friend Who Didn't Arrive Because of Heavy Rain" (p. 34)
    Eight five-character lines.
    Title: *Qi you ren zu yu bu zhi*
    First line: *Yan yu kong you xin*

For the geese and fish, see note on "Early Autumn," p. 31. Note the progression outward and then suddenly back to the poem itself.

"Visiting Master Zhao and Not Finding Him" (p. 35)
    Eight five-character lines.
    Title: *Fang Zhao lian shi bu yu*
    First line: *He chu tong xian lü*

Poems about visiting hermits and not finding them home were a kind of sub-genre in this period. This compares with the best of them. Zhao is an alchemist, like the one admired in "Tribute to a Master Alchemist," p. 4. The boy servant is not literally mentioned; it is "someone dressed in dark blue." We know from the clothing that it is a member of the working poor.

"Curing Yourself When Lovesick" (p. 36)
>Sixteen five-character lines.
>Title: *Qian huai*
>First line: *Xian san shen wu shi*

There are several specific allusions in this poem. The Liang Dynasty (502–557) was ruled by the House of Xiao, so the poem speaks of "Xiao Liang" temples. The next line puns on this reference by invoking Yu Liang (289–340), a prime minister of the Jin Dynasty (317–420). The general idea seems to be that of learning to enjoy the fruits of the past, becoming a sort of antiquarian aesthete. This joins with an idealization of retreat from the world and closeness to nature.

"Sent to Feiqing" (p. 38)
>Eight five-character lines.
>Title: *Ji Fei qing*
>First line: *Jie qi luan qiong ming*

The second poem addressed to this well-known poet, whose real name was Wen Tingyun. The philosopher mentioned in the next to last couplet is Ji Kang (224–263), of the Three Kingdoms era (220–280).

"Visiting Ezhou" (p. 39)
>Eight seven-character lines.
>Title: *Guo E zhou*
>First line: *Liu fu lan nao hua man zhi*

This poem is laced with culture-specific allusions. Ezhou is part of Wuhan city. "Stone City" probably refers to Nanjing, nicknamed "the city of stone walls." Qu Yuan (343–289 B.C.) is here actually referred to by his "style name," Sanlü. The magistrate's carriage is a five-horse affair, indicating the governor of a prefecture.

"Living in the Mountains in Summer" (p. 40)
>Eight seven-character lines.
>Title: *Xia ri shan ju*
>First line: *Yi de xian ju ci di lai*

A celebration of solitude, peace and rural enchantment.

"Late Spring Improvisation" (p. 41)
Eight seven-character lines.
Title: *Mu chun ji shi*
First line: *Shen xiang qiong men shao lü chou*

A plaintive counterpart to the previous poem. Here the emphasis is on being left out of the world of men and fame.

"Joining Somebody's Mourning" (p. 42)
Eight seven-character lines.
Title: *Dai ren dao wang*
First line: *Ceng du yao tao xiang yu zi*

The title seems to suggest that the poet is commemorating the life and mourning the death of someone she knew only slightly and was not related to, a beautiful woman who has died young.

"Letter to a Friend" (p. 43)
Eight seven-character lines.
Title: *He ren*
First line: *Mang mang jiu mo wu zhi ji*

Something of a self-portrait. The incense burner is specified as "Boshan style," famous for its intricate carving. The famous beauties are represented by Zhuo Wenjun.

"Sent to Zian, Long Distance, from the Hanjiang River" (p. 44)
Eight six-character lines, an unusual variation.
Title: *Ge Han jiang ji Zi an*
First line: *Jiang nan jiang bei chou wang*

The poem suggests that a psychological or spiritual distance has grown up that is more significant than the physical distance.

"An Allegory" (p. 45)
> Eight six-character lines, another unusual six-character variation.
> Title: *Yu yan*
> First line: *Hong tao chu chu chun se*

> The last lines feel personal, a summary of the poet's own existence.

"Letter to Zian, Sad from Gazing into the Distance, from Jiangling" (p. 46)
> Four seven-character lines.
> Title: *Jiang ling chou wang ji Zi an*
> First line: *Feng ye qian zhi fu wan zhi*

> Again, conventional images of loss and change, powerfully deployed.

"Sent to Zian" (p. 47)
> Eight seven-character lines.
> Title: *Ji Zi an*
> First line: *Zui bie qian zhi bu huan chou*

> The wine-flowers-willow-clouds pattern of imagery here is a characteristic cluster of associations in Chinese poetry.

"Saying Goodbye" (p. 48)
> Four seven-character lines.
> Title: *Song bie*
> First line: *Qin lou ji ye qie xin qi*

> Like the poem on p. 46, "Letter to Zian, Sad . . . ," this demonstrates the poet's gift for exact succinctness.

"A Warm Note to Squire Li Jinren" (p. 49)
> Four seven-character lines.
> Title: *Ying Li Jin ren yuan wai*
> First line: *Jin ri xi shi wen xi que*

The third line compares her guest to the handsome poet Pan Yue, of the Western Jin Dynasty (A.D. 265–316). The Weaver Girl and the Cowherd were the names for two stars, Vega and Altair respectively, representing two faithful, separated lovers. They met once a year by crossing the Milky Way (in China, *yin he*, the Silver River), so of course they were only a happy couple a small percentage of the time.

"Saying Goodbye, II" (p. 50)

    Four seven-character lines.

    Title: *Song bie*

    First line: *Shui rou zhu qi zhi nan ding*

We've used "Yangtze" for the great river now known more properly as Changjiang River because this name is so familiar to Western readers. Actually, because of the river's great length (Changjiang means "long river"), it tended to be referred to in terms of its specific sections. In this poem Yu Xuanji refers to the Chujiang River section. Because the title is exactly the same in Chinese as the title of the poem on p. 48, we have added the number.

"Letter to an Exam Candidate, from Shanxi to the Capital" (p. 51)

    Twelve seven-character lines.

    Title: *Zuo ming chang zi Ze zhou zhi jing shi ren chuan yu*

    First line: *Xian ju zuo fu ji nian chou*

Zezhou is in Shanxi Province. The Wangwu Mountains are some fifty miles north of the ancient capital, Luoyang. Sima Xiangru (179–117 B.C.) was a Western Han Dynasty poet. The "White Dew," marking the advent of autumn, was said to come about 15 days before the autumnal equinox. The Yangtze Delta is the Qujiang River section.

"Reply to a Poem, Matching the Form" (p. 53)

    Eight seven-character lines.

    Title: *He ren ci yun*

    First line: *Xuan xuan zhu zi za ren huan*

A kind of summing up. Yan Yuan (521–490 B.C.) was a disciple of Confucius, praised for his humility and contentment.

"Three Beautiful Sisters, Orphaned Young" (p. 54)

Twenty four seven-character lines.

Title: *Guang Wei Pou jie mei san ren, shao gu er shi yan, nai you shi zuo, jing cui nan chou, sui Xie jia lian [ ], he yi jia zhi, you ke zi jing shi lai zhe shi yu, yin ci qi yun*

First line: *Xi wen nan guo rong hua shao*

The unusual title of this poem translates in full as: "Three Sisters, Guang, Wei, and Pou, Young as Orphans and Now Contending in Beauty, So to Have This Poem, Succinct and Terse, Hard to Compare, Even If the Xie Family [one character missing], What Way to Enhance, Some Visitor Coming from the Capital, Showing It to Me, Allowing Me to Compose a Poem in Reply."

The poet seems to have been shown a poem celebrating these three beautiful sisters and to have composed her own response, meditating on the way women tended to be reduced to questions of beauty and marriageability in her society.

The section breaks have been introduced here to clarify the movement of the poem. In the second section, the poet mentioned is Cai Wenji (active around 190), an Eastern Han Dynasty woman poet, and the famous beauty is Xi Shi, from the fifth century B.C. (see "Washing Yarn Temple," p. 7). Xi Shi was admirable, but it is ironic, the poet suggests, that a woman poet gets compared to other women and praised for beauty rather than to other (male) poets.

The young poet's dream-lover in the third section is Pan Yue, who seems to have been her prototype for the dashing, handsome poet-lover.

In its bitterness and inclusiveness, this poem stands out from the rest of Yu Xuanji's work.

"Snapping Willows" (p. 57)

Four seven-character lines.

Title: *Zhe yang liu*

First line: *Zhao zhao song bie qi hua dian*

The association of willows with parting probably came about because it was typical to see someone off on a journey by accompanying them to the town or city gates. There would be a stream or river there, with willows growing beside it. Breaking off a branch or wand would commemorate the occasion. The drooping look of the tree also gives it associations of melancholy, of course, and in Western traditions it has become closely associated with disappointed lovers.

"Fragments." (p. 58)

The first four are each two five-character lines, and the fifth is two seven-charac-ter lines.

Title: *Ju*

First line: *Fen xiang deng yu tan*

These seem to be pairs of lines that were actual or potential parts of complete poems. They were presumably admired enough in this incomplete form to be considered worth including in the collection of Yu Xuanji's surviving works.

About the Translators

David Young is Longman Professor of English and the Humanities at Oberlin College. He has published eight volumes of poetry over thirty years, including *The Planet on the Desk: Selected and New Poems* (Wesleyan, 1991), and numerous translations, including *Five T'ang Poets: Wang Wei, Li Po, Tu Fu, Li Ho and Li Shang-yin* (Oberlin College Press, the *FIELD* Translation Series, 1991).

Jiann I. Lin was born in Taiwan and emigrated to the United States in 1963. He was educated at National Taiwan University, the University of Wisconsin–Madison, and the State University of New York at Albany. He is East Asian Specialist Librarian at Oberlin College Library, responsible for the management and operation of Oberlin's East Asian Collection in Chinese and Japanese.

About the Author

Yu Xuanji (ca. 844–ca. 871) is among the most gifted and original poets of the late Tang Dynasty. Her short life (twenty-eight years, according to Chinese custom) and her uncertain moral status (she was executed on the accusation of having killed her maid), along with her gender, have contributed to an undeserved obscurity that has begun to reverse itself in the twentieth century, although her work is still not widely known. This is the first complete rendering in English of her small poetic canon.

Library of Congress Cataloging-in-Publication Data
Yü, Hsüan-chi, 842–872.
    [Poems. English]
    The clouds float north : the complete poems of Yu Xuanji / translated by David Young and Jiann I. Lin. — Bilingual ed.
    p. cm. — (Wesleyan poetry)
    ISBN 0–8195–6343–9 (alk. paper). — ISBN 0–8195–6344–7 (pbk. : alk. paper)
    1. Yü, Hsüan-chi, 842–872.—Translations into English. I. Young, David. II. Lin, Jiann I. III. Title. IV. Title: Complete Poems of Yu Xuanji V. Series.
PL2677.Y77A28 1998   98–22527
895.1'13—dc21